D0890048

WITHDRAWN

THEY KNEW WHAT THEY WANTED

JOHN ASHBERY

THEY KNEW WHAT THEY WANTED

POEMS & COLLAGES

edited by Mark Polizzotti

introduction and interview by John Yau

RIZZOLI Electa

Contents

Preface

Max Ernst cannily remarked that "it's not the *colle* [paste] that makes the collage." Rather, as he and so many other modernist paragons knew full well, it's the thought behind all that scissoring and gluing, the choice and arrangement of elements, the savvy collusions and chance associations, the proverbial whole that becomes more than the sum.

Inspired by the spirit of assemblage that animates so much of John Ashbery's work, this volume aims to create juxtapositions of words and images that will highlight their own collusions and associations, and perhaps offer ways of appreciating these remarkable pieces in a new light. Though the works speak for themselves, readers wishing to know more about Ashbery's approach to collage will find it in the illuminating interview by John Yau. I would merely add that the poems have been arranged in chronological order (publication dates are given on page 127), with the collages acting as visual and thematic counterpoints, in a sustained call-and-response between the two media.

One note, though: while the collage principle is self-evident in the visual creations, it might be less so in the poems. Many of Ashbery's writings incorporate fragments — his own or others' — to achieve a particular effect through accretion and abutment, but the process is enacted in many different ways, not all of them clear-cut. Poems such as "Hoboken," "Europe," or the recently discovered "'controls,'" for instance, openly demonstrate the collagist impulse, but "Daffy Duck in Hollywood," though it, too, pulls together disparate elements and references as if grabbing them pell-mell from the ambient air, maintains a more identifiable narrative flow. Others employ restrictive forms as a collaborative spur: Centos ("The Dong with the Luminous Nose") are made entirely of lines lifted from other poets; pantoums and sestinas ("Pantoum," "Farm Implements and Rutabagas in a Landscape") use strictly regulated patterns of repetition to guide the generative process; "Finnish Rhapsody" is based on a traditional Finnish form in which the first phrase of each line is paraphrased by the second. The poem "They Knew What They Wanted" is composed exclusively of film titles beginning with the word "they." "The Songs We Know Best" borrows its rhythm and structure from the 1978 Peaches & Herb hit "Reunited" (try singing it — it works!). And so on.

Needless to say, these poems and collages are not the only forms in which Ashbery has exercised his passion for juxtapositions. As David Kermani wrote to me, John's "creative processes have involved these concepts from the beginning, whether constructing playhouses from found materials with his childhood friends or creating the environment that's his Hudson house; his lifelong collecting of the bits and pieces that he eventually uses to create his physical surroundings, poems, and collages; or his collaborations both with others and with the objects and materials from which he fashions new work and environments." Without belaboring the point, I'll also note that André Breton likened Ernst's collage volumes *La Femme 100 têtes* and *Une semaine de bonté* to a "child's first picture-book," foregrounding the collage's undertones of innocent mischief, irreverent humor, and endless wonder that are the privileged capacities of the childlike mind, and that, if we're lucky, never abandon us.

Simply put, the collage aesthetic, in all its variety and breadth, is central to any understanding of John Ashbery's body of work. It is this variety, and the remarkable energy that derives from it, that I have sought to highlight in the pages that follow.

— *Mark Polizzotti, August 2017*

POSTSCRIPT

This book was about to go press when John Ashbery passed away, at his home in Hudson, New York, on the morning of September 3, 2017. While he had been involved in the project during the nearly ten years of its preparation, and had reviewed and approved the final layouts, it will always be my deep regret that he was not able to see a copy of the finished work.

These introductory texts, written while John was still alive, naturally speak of him in the present tense. Because this volume was for all intents and purposes finished before his passing, we decided to keep them as they are, reflecting both a vital collaboration and an ongoing inquiry into this remarkable portion of his oeuvre.

They Knew What They Wanted is dedicated to John Ashbery, with gratitude.

Introduction

I first met John Ashbery in 1975, and we have been friends for more than forty years. During that time, we have gone to the movies, attended recitals and operas, heard poetry readings, had dinners, gone to parties, ridden the subway, taken taxis, sat in cars being driven somewhere, watched television, looked at art in galleries and museums, browsed flea markets, estate sales, and antique stores, visited different cities and countries together. One summer, as the result of a conversation John had with my wife, Eve Aschheim, we met him and David Kermani in Paris and drove them to the seaside resort of Cabourg to spend the night at Le Grand Hôtel.

Immortalized by Marcel Proust, who came to Cabourg every summer from 1907 to 1914, the luxury hotel overlooks a pristine stretch of sand and gently rolling waves, with its famed gourmet restaurant adjacent to the boardwalk. As we explored the hotel, John pointed to different photographs of stars and singers of a bygone era lining one of the many hallways. It seemed as if he knew something about each and every one of them. When he saw the ornate escritoire in his room, he said, ironically and instinctually, "I think I will write a poem." Over dinner, which was brought to us on covered silver trays, John recalled passages from Proust's monumental masterpiece, *A la recherche du temps perdu*, until, as often happens in the book, the present succumbed to the past. One quote he recalled described the boulevardiers strolling along the boardwalk and peering into the elegant restaurant as if they were looking into a fishbowl. Suddenly, it seemed as if we were both inside and outside the fishbowl, looking at the people looking in. A Proustian scene slowly grew around us, filtered through John's memory and imagination. Time — past and present — collapsed into a series of magical moments, like one of John's collages.

This interview is a composite of conversations John and I had at various times over a ten-year period, always with the main subject being his collages. The conversations took place at his apartment on the ninth floor of a nondescript postwar building in Manhattan, and at his Colonial Revival house in Hudson, New York. During the many visits I paid to his airy Manhattan apartment, where the windows face west, south, and east, I became well acquainted with his collection of nineteenth-century French puzzle-plates, with their interlaced words and images, side by side with artwork by Joe Brainard, Jane Freilicher, Anne Dunn, Anne Ryan, Leland Bell, and Trevor Winkfield, among others, not to mention his toy figurines and the head of Popeye popping out of a can of spinach. They all came together like an Ashbery poem.

John's Colonial Revival house has many rooms, all of which are filled with eye-catching stuff, from paintings to lithographs to postcards. In an article about the house, Rosanne Wasserman wrote:

> Ashbery once mentioned to me that his arrangements of objects follow various dramas in his imagination: in part a re-creation of his grandparents' home in Rochester, New York, where he spent much of his childhood; and in part an idea of what might exist in each room, in some dreamed-up family, as if he were designing a stage set, a giant dollhouse, or a gargantuan Cornell box.[*]

John's collages were always nearby wherever and whenever we talked, marking the trail as our conversation wandered off in a hundred directions. His mind is a vast domain of unlikely associations, of little-known facts and memories, all effortlessly accessible anytime he needs them. I can't think of a time when we were together that he has not recalled something surprising and unlikely. Fortunately, many of John's insights and anecdotes have been preserved on tape, and from all the recorded material I have gathered over the years, I put together this record as a definitive account of our conversations. I would like to think it gets at the heart of what it is like to talk with John.

— *John Yau, June 2017*

---

[*] Roseanne Wasserman, "Hudson 1993: A Tour of John Ashbery's Home" can be found, along with many other wonderful essays about John's domestic spaces, on the *Rain Taxi* website.

John Yau: Before we talk about your collages, I thought we should provide people with a little background. You grew up in upstate New York on a farm outside Rochester. The farm was just outside Sodus, which is near the shore of Lake Ontario, between Rochester and Syracuse. In 1933, when you were six, you saw your first film, *The Three Little Pigs* and, shortly after that, *Alice in Wonderland*.

John Ashbery: Yes, although I was recently looking at the release dates of those movies on IMDb [Internet Movie Database], and I'm a little confused about the chronology. My recollection was that *The Three Little Pigs* was on the same bill with *Bring 'Em Back Alive*, by Frank Buck, an explorer and exhibitor of wild animals who was very famous in the '30s. I thought that would've been early in 1933 and that I immediately saw *Alice in Wonderland* a week or so later, but it turns out *Alice in Wonderland* wasn't released until Christmas 1933. Anyway, I don't know that it matters very much. It doesn't [*laughs*]. But *Alice in Wonderland* was the first, you know, adult movie I ever saw — it's far from a movie for adults, though it is a rather creepy version of the story. I mean, unintentionally, in large part. It had sort of German Expressionist touches. It starred Charlotte Henry, W. C. Fields, Cary Grant, Gary Cooper, Edna May Oliver, Edward Everett Horton, and Baby LeRoy. William Cameron Menzies had something to do with the visuals, and he co-wrote the screenplay. You probably know that he also did the sets for *The Thief of Baghdad* and for *Gone with the Wind;* the famous scenes where Atlanta is burning are his.

JY: This seems to be the beginning of your love of movies. Did you see a lot of movies at that age, when you were six and seven?

JA: Well, not as many as I wanted. I was only allowed to see children's movies, like the ones Shirley Temple was in — *The Littlest Rebel* and *Bright Eyes*. But I was reading about other movies in the newspapers by then, and I even got hold of movie magazines.

JY: Okay, so at the age of six, you saw your first movie and began reading about them in the newspapers and movie magazines. This deep interest in movies has been there ever since your childhood. Since you were reading the newspaper, what about comic strips? Which ones do you most remember reading? Did you look at them on the weekend?

JA: Yes, on the weekend the funnies were in color, as you know. I read *Popeye.*

JY: What about the *Katzenjammer Kids,* with the twins Hans and Fritz?

JA: That didn't come out in the Rochester paper. Our relatives from Buffalo would descend on us at the farm for the weekend, and they brought movie magazines with them — that's how I got them. My father's cousins, Betty and Lois, would bring the Buffalo paper, which had the *Katzenjammer Kids,* which I always looked forward to intensely. I also liked *Toots and Casper* — they were newlyweds who had a child, Buttercup, and a pet dog, Spare-Rib. *The Gumps* and *The Nebbs* — two all-American families. *Winnie Winkle*, about a secretary who supports her parents and adopted brother, and a rival lass, *Somebody's Stenog.* And a golf strip, *Divot Diggers.* And *Mickey Finn.* And *Simp O'Dill.* Can you believe there was a comic called *Simp O'Dill?*

JY: Along with reading comic strips and about movies, in 1936, when you were nine, you learned about the show "Fantastic Art: Dada and Surrealism" in *Life* magazine. After reading about the show, which was at the Museum of Modern Art in New York, you decided you wanted to be a surrealist painter. In 1936, surrealism was still news, especially in America, and you were reading about it as a nine-year-old, thinking, "Oh, I want to be a surrealist painter." Were you drawing and painting a lot at this point in your life?

JA: Yes, I was. David discovered a big envelope of my childhood drawings just the other day. My mother had put them in an envelope and labeled it. The drawings are from before I started taking a children's art class, which I did with my brother, at the Memorial Art Gallery, the Rochester art museum, in the fall of 1938, when I was eleven. As I recall, they had stopped teaching art at the Sodus public school because of budget woes, the same story as today. So I got permission to take Friday afternoon off from school and ride with my parents to the big city, where my father sold eggs and other stuff from the farm to a restaurant, actually a glorified soda fountain, where we would have dinner, or "supper," after our event-filled afternoon. I think I continued the class until the spring of 1943.

In September of 1943 — my senior year in high school — I went to Deerfield Academy, a boarding school in Deerfield, Massachusetts. It was rare to transfer that late. At

NAPOLEON, 2009 (12.375 x 9.175 in.)

the end of the school year, they talked me into staying another year, so I got out in 1945. This was because they said I was too young for college — I had skipped a grade when I was in elementary school and was seventeen. I really wasn't very happy at Deerfield that first year, but it turned out I enjoyed my second year much more.

JY: You began taking art classes when you were eleven. When did you start writing poetry?

JA: Aside from some childhood attempts, I started doing that when I was about fifteen, and I won a prize in a *Time* current events contest. *Time* magazine used to have these contests for high school students whose class subscribed to *Time* magazine, and the winner would get a prize of a book. I was offered three different books, none of which interested me very much, but I chose Louis Untermeyer's anthology of *Modern American and Modern British Poetry* — a combined edition —since it seemed the least uninteresting of the three. But then I began reading modern poetry and getting very interested in it, and every week when we went to Rochester for the art class I'd go to the public library — they have a wonderful, very beautiful public library there, it's still there, built in the '30s, Deco. And they had a terrific literature section, especially contemporary poetry.

JY: Which poets were you reading then?

JA: Well, a lot of the poets of the '30s who were very avant-garde, but nobody seems to remember them much. There was Delmore Schwartz — he was the best. I liked his work a lot.

JY: Didn't you meet Schwartz later?

JA: Yes. He was the poetry editor of *Partisan Review,* and he took one of my poems shortly after I moved to New York — around 1950. That was a big thrill. My first major publication, although I had been in a magazine called *Furioso* while I was still in college.

JY: And you were reading W. H. Auden.

JA: Yes, Auden. And I always read the poems in the annual Oscar Williams anthologies. Another poet who was very big at that time was Dunstan Thompson. Did you ever read him? He has recently been rediscovered.

Let's see, one particularly good poet was named Ruth Herschberger, and another was Jean Garrigue. There were also Weldon Kees and Nicholas Moore. I read Moore in *Poetry* magazine and other American poetry magazines, and I think maybe they had books of his at the Rochester library. I remember he won one of the prizes from *Poetry* one year, so he was quite well known in America.

JY: Didn't you also go to antique and curio shops in Rochester with your friend Mary Wellington? And weren't you reading about English houses around this time, when you were fifteen and sixteen?

JA: Yes, I used to go to antique shops with Mary, and I guess there are letters I wrote to her about going to the curio shop in Rochester, which we used to do. I did read about English houses then. The other day, David and I were watching the English *Antiques Roadshow,* which they have at a different building every week — a castle or an English public building. And there was this one called Kedleston, which I remembered as being one of the great English Palladian houses. And I said, "Oh, that's Kedleston," and David said, "How did you know about that?" I said, "Well, I used to read books about English architecture." Basically, I wanted to live in an English manor house, rather than on a crappy farm with the house we were living in, though my family did have some lovely Oriental tchotchkes.

JY: Was this the beginning of your interest in objets d'art?

JA: Probably. Most of them were brought back by my grandparents from their one trip to Europe and the Middle East in the mid-1920s, and they were in their house in Rochester, where I spent a lot of time as a child.

JY: Did you take art classes while you were at Deerfield?

JA: There was a painting studio, which was not actually part of the curriculum, but was sort of optional. If you wanted to go there and work with the artist- and painter-in-residence, you could do that. We were all called fairies because of this, although only some of us were [*laughs*]. The art studio was presided over by a local artist named Donald Greason, who had lived in Paris in the twenties, where he shared a studio with Alexander Calder. He was a talented — more than that, actually — painter in what today would be called the painterly realist tradition. He told me it was okay to be a surrealist, but first I had to learn to draw and paint "things as they are," to quote Wallace Stevens. So I did still-lifes from the models and even a self-portrait (now lost), and got quite caught up in it. Every week a painting was chosen and it got displayed in the headmaster's office, and mine got hung a few times. I had a close friend, Gillett Griffin, who was a gifted artist (a "good drawer"), and who later became a curator of Pre-Columbian and Native American art at the Princeton University Art Museum. He died in 2016. He made some important discoveries. Gillett was passionate about Greason's work, and even bought a house in the same hilltop village of Colrain, Massachusetts, where he lived.

JY: Do you remember when you first went to the Museum of Modern Art?

JA: I went on my first trip to New York, in my second year at Deerfield. This was in December 1944. My parents allowed me to come to New York by myself, and I stayed in the Roosevelt Hotel. I went to the Broadway Theatre on my own, too, and saw *Carmen Jones*, which I had heard the recording of. The music was by Georges Bizet, and the lyrics were by Oscar Hammerstein. It had an all-black cast. It was very exciting. I also saw Gillett, who came into New York from Greenwich, Connecticut, where his parents lived.

JY: Do you remember when you first started making collages?

JA: It wasn't until I got to Harvard. I graduated from Deerfield in June 1945, two months before the end of World War II. I think I could have gotten into any college because they were all empty. I got into Harvard, which I never could've done today. According to Karin Roffman, who has written a book about my early life,[*] I first mention collages in a diary entry in the spring of 1948, near the end of the semester, which means when I was twenty. One entry says something like, "I woke up with a cold today, made a lovely collage." And then a couple of weeks later, when I had gotten back to Sodus because I couldn't find a summer job in New York, I wrote in my diary that I dreamed about collage. It is likely that I began making collages before these diary entries.

JY: What got you to start making them around 1948?

---

[*] Karin Roffman, *The Songs We Know Best: John Ashbery's Early Life* (New York: Farrar, Straus & Giroux, 2017).

JA: There was a collage show at MoMA in the fall of '48, which I don't think I saw, but I might have read an article about it, maybe in *Vogue*. I think I remember seeing the Max Ernst one of a woman, which is actually made of a spool of embroidery thread. But it's possible that the article about the fall '48 collage show was what got me started doing it then. I might have made some before, but I don't remember that. Although, come to think of it, I had seen surrealist collages, I think also in *Vogue,* in my dentist's office when I was about twelve years old. I remember thinking that those wouldn't be all that difficult to do, and they looked kind of fun.

JY: And how many did you make?

JA: I can't remember. I think I made quite a lot. I don't know, maybe twenty.

JY: Were you collecting pictures then? I mean, postcards and stuff like that? You have always had an incredible visual memory of the things that you'd seen or saw reproductions of. And there were all those secondhand bookstores in Cambridge, which must have been heavenly.

JA: When I started making collages, I found some nineteenth-century German children's books at Schoenhof's, which used to be on Mass. Avenue in Harvard Square. There is a collage that I titled *Late for School* that I did around this time. I remember using photographs from *Vogue*. I also did one with a photograph of Proust in it, which I think I still have somewhere. It had been at my parents' house. I did it just after I began reading Proust, which was around then. Unfortunately, a lot of my collages got thrown out when my mother sold our house in the 1960s and moved, and I wasn't there to help her, which is my punishment, I guess. My aunt saved it and gave it to me.

JY: You read Proust in translation in the beginning. Did you later read him in French?

JA: Yes, parts of him.

JY: So you went to stores like that and bought stuff, which had nothing to do with your studies, with the purpose of making collages?

JA: Right, although in my freshman year I had a twentieth-century art course, which included Max Ernst. I remember particularly one slide in the course, a collage called *The Hat Makes the Man* (1920), made of advertisements for men's hats. Another work I recall from that course is Ernst's painting *Garden Airplane Trap* (c. 1936).

JY: So you took two art history courses at Harvard, one obviously on twentieth-century art, before you started making collages. What was the other course?

JA: The other course was on Northern European painting of the Renaissance.

JY: You studied the work of Hans Holbein and others?

JA: Yes.

JY: In the collage on the cover of the *Harvard Advocate* in November 1948 — the first time one of your collages was reproduced — there is a reproduction of Holbein's *Portrait of Anne of Cleves* (c. 1539). Didn't you also paint that as a child, copying it from a book or something?

JA: As you know, Holbein painted the portrait of Anne on parchment so that Henry VIII could see if he wanted to marry her. We had a print of it in the living room, and I copied it from that and painted it on some unbleached muslin. I did it in the summer, in August 1939. I still have that painting, actually. It's rather pathetic [*laughs*].

JY: So you made a number of collages in 1948, some of which survived, and one of them was used on the cover of the *Harvard Advocate* — a collaboration with your friend Fred Amory. And then in 1949 you moved to New York.

JA: Yes, I came to New York after I graduated from Harvard and got a job at the Brooklyn Public Library for the summer — an unrewarding job — and I met Jane Freilicher at the same time. Kenneth Koch, whom I met at Harvard, said I could stay at his place while he was away visiting his parents. Jane lived in the same building and had the key to let me in. It was a three-story walk-up on Third Avenue between 16th and 17th overlooking the El, which rattled by regularly. Kenneth used to put on a rubber ape mask and look out of the window as the train passed.

NOVEMBER ISSUE, 1948

35c

Harvard Advocate

HARVARD ADVOCATE COVER, 1948

SEAPORT, CA. 1948 (10.5 x 8 IN.)

LATE FOR SCHOOL, CA. 1948 (12.5 x 8 IN.)

In order to get the job at the Brooklyn Library, I had to pledge to go to library school at Columbia. I was sick of the job after a few weeks. Finally, I got accepted at Columbia graduate school, but was turned down by Harvard. At the end of the summer I had to go and tell the library that I would be going to graduate school and that I would be leaving the job. I expected them to make a huge fuss, but actually they were quite pleased. "Oh, that's nice!" [*Laughs.*] So in the fall of 1949, I started Columbia with the idea of getting a master's in English. I was living in Greenwich Village all this time, at different places, and then I managed to stretch the M.A. out for another year, and my parents grumblingly paid for it.

JY: This must be when you started reading Henry Green, because isn't that what your M.A. thesis was about?

JA: Yes, I found this bookstore on East 55th Street. It was called the Periscope Bookstore, and they had a lot of English imports. That's where I first happened on Henry Green, Ivy Compton-Burnett, and other writers. So I decided to do my M.A. thesis on Green. There was a professor at Columbia, William York Tindall. He was a James Joyce scholar, the first in America, I believe. He also wrote a scholarly book on British fiction. He was sort of a pill, actually. I was also reading Ronald Firbank then, because New Directions had recently published his *Five Novels*.

JY: I don't think that Firbank would have gone over in the English department at Columbia [*laughs*].

JA: No, he wouldn't have. In fact, in his book on twentieth-century English fiction, Tindall only mentions Firbank in a footnote, which was, "He was a corrupt dandy who wrote verbal arabesques." And it happened at that time that W. H. Auden reviewed *Five Novels* on the front page of the *New York Times Book Review,* so the next time I saw Tindall I said, "Well, did you see Auden's review of Firbank?" Tindall said, "Well, yes, but I think that's a case of homosexual calling to homosexual across the abyss." I was tempted to say, "I'm glad you think it's an abyss!" [*Laughter.*] Unfortunately, I didn't.

JY: Did you make collages when you came to New York? You knew quite a few artists, like Larry Rivers and Jane Freilicher.

JA: It's possible that I made some more, but I don't remember — I don't think I did. It probably had something to do with, you know, moving to New York and trying to figure out my life in the city. I used to hang out with some people at the Phoenix Book Shop when it was on Cornelia Street and owned by someone named Adam. This was long before Robert Wilson (not *the* Robert Wilson) owned it. Adam was friends with a guy I knew named John Lynch, whom I shared an apartment with at some point. They were friends with Ann Truxell — I don't know if you've ever heard of her. She was a painter who got to be rather well known; she did very sort of kooky, neo-primitive paintings. We would sit around and do abstract paintings in the Phoenix Book Shop. I did some pseudo-Pollocks at that time, which unfortunately haven't survived.

JY: So you were still making art, in other words, after you got to New York.

JA: Actually not. I don't think I really did any. Except for maybe, you know, the handful of things that I did at the Phoenix.

JY: When was this?

JA: 1949, '50, and '51. But I really only did a few things at the Phoenix Book Shop.

JY: And this group — Adam, John Lynch, and Ann Truxell — was separate from the social scene to which Jane Freilicher, Kenneth Koch, and O'Hara belonged?

JA: Yes, they knew each other, but they were separate.

JY: Were you going to galleries then?

JA: I was. And then, when Frank O'Hara moved to New York, which was in the fall of '51, he was much more clued in to the current art scene than I was. We used to go to art shows together. I remember Jackson Pollock, Mark Rothko, Joseph Cornell, and others. I would go to the galleries — Betty Parsons, Sidney Janis, Charles Egan. And, of course, Tibor de Nagy, which had just opened.

JY: Did you also go to the Cedar Bar with Frank?

JA: I did some, although I never really got to know any of those people. And I don't think they knew who I was: I was this person who tagged along with Frank.

JY: What were you doing for a living?

JA: When I got my M.A., I was supposed to get a teaching job, but of course I didn't. I applied for one at Lehigh University in Pennsylvania, but was turned down there. I probably applied elsewhere, too, as I was trying to get any job that I could. Finally, I got a job at Oxford University Press as, well, basically, a typist. I typed out labels for review copies and eventually I was sort of elevated to writing jacket copy and press releases.

JY: When did you meet Jimmy Schuyler?

JA: 1951, I think. It was my second year in New York.

JY: But then you made some collages in 1952, after you and Schuyler saw a Kurt Schwitters show. You mention this in a chatty letter — which included a collage poem — that you sent to Robert Fizdale.*

JA: Oh, I don't know if those collages count.

JY: Was the collage poem you sent to Fizdale the first collage poem that you wrote?

JA: Probably not, but there weren't many.

JY: Let me get this straight. By 1952, you had made around twenty collages and written at least a few poems using collage techniques.

JA: Yeah.

JY: Along with making collages with Jimmy one afternoon, the two of you wrote a novel together. How did that start?

*See the poem "'controls'" in this volume.

JA: We started that in '52, while coming back from Long Island. The first time I went there, we were given a ride back by Harrison Starr, who was working on a film about Jane Freilicher called *Presenting Jane*. Jimmy had written a scenario for it. So Harrison and his father were in the front of the car, and Jimmy and I were rather bored in the back. And I said, "What'll we do? This is so boring." And he said, "Why don't we write a novel?" And I said, "Well, that's good. How do we do that?" He said, "It's easy. You write the first line." Typical of him. So I wrote the first sentence, which was, "Alice was tired." And we went on for two or three pages on that car trip. That was in 1952. We'd get together occasionally to work on it. We found we had to be in the same room together; we couldn't do it by correspondence, meaning we weren't able to work on it at all while I was living in France between 1955 and '65. Eventually, my editor, Arthur Cohen, asked me — as most editors of poets do — "Did you ever think about writing a novel?" I said, "Well, yes, I think I did start one maybe a long time *ago* . . ." So he urged me to continue working on it. Which we did. And eventually *A Nest of Ninnies* got written and was published in 1968.

JY: In 1955, after working as a copy editor for four years, you got a Fulbright fellowship and went to France, where you stayed for ten years, first in Montpellier and Rennes. Before you went to France, didn't Fairfield Porter try to get you to paint again?

JA: Yes, I painted *Mantelpiece* (1955) in Porter's home in Southampton.

JY: After living in Montpellier and Rennes, you moved to Paris in 1958. This is when you continued experimenting with cut-ups and collage in your poems, partially because you felt isolated from America and its language. You lived there until you returned to New York in 1965. While living in Paris, you wrote art criticism for the European edition of the *New York Herald Tribune, Art International,* and *Art News,* as well as co-translating French murder mysteries, using the pseudonym Jonas Berry — which is how a Frenchman would pronounce your name. You began a dissertation on the then little-known writer Raymond Roussel. You interviewed the reclusive writer and artist Henri Michaux, and translated works by Giorgio de Chirico, Max Jacob, and Pierre Reverdy. In fact, you translated a lot of Reverdy's work while you were living in Paris and have continued to do so. Did you meet him while you were there?

JA: No, by that time he had moved to Solesmes, to be near the famous Benedictine Abbey of Saint-Pierre de Solesmes.

JY: Did you make any collages while you were in Paris?

JA: No, I didn't make any art. Did you know that Pierre Martory, whom I was living with in Paris, and whose poems I translated, made collages?*

JY: Did Pierre make a lot of collages, or just a few?

JA: Quite a few.

JY: And do you have any of them?

JA: Yes, well, one of them, and it's sitting framed back in Manhattan.

JY: In the mid 1960s, when your father died, you moved back to New York, and in the early 1970s you began making collages again.

JY: In the '70s, during the summer, we'd be invited up to Kenward [Elmslie]'s place in Vermont, and after dinner we'd stay up late making collages. Me, Joe Brainard, Jimmy Schuyler. A lot of those were in my first solo show at the Tibor de Nagy Gallery. The ones that were dated in the early to mid-'70s were from Kenward's.

JY: And Kenward was a big postcard collector, too. Did he supply the postcards?

JA: Yes. I remember one of them that I made there, a postcard of some mountains in the background, and in the foreground is a man's head, wearing a hat, looking very evil.

JY: By the time you began making collages again, you had written about Joseph Cornell and Anne Ryan, both of whom made collages. In fact, you once owned a collage by Cornell and have one by Anne Ryan. It is made of pieces of fabric and cloth. She was around fifty when she began making collages. In 1970, when you wrote about an exhibition of Ryan's at a gallery, you began with an autobiographical anecdote, which reads:

---

*The translations were published as *The Landscapist: Selected Poems of Pierre Martory* (Rhinebeck, NY: Sheep Meadow Press, 2008).

Tramping Party and Mts. Clay, Jefferson and Adams, White Mts., N. H.

TRAMPING PARTY, 1972 (3.5 x 5.5 IN.)

When I was a small child there was a box in the attic containing neatly trimmed scraps of material that had once belonged to dresses, aprons, blouses, dishtowels, and which were apparently intended for a quilt that never got made. I was fascinated by them and used to pore over them with the zeal of an Egyptologist. There was a language there.

To me, it's interesting that you don't stop there, but go on, looking more intently at what you see.

The fact that certain dots were so close together that they took up more space than the colored ground; the way the stripes in gingham went over or under each other to make checks; the way the prickly flowers nudged each other; the way a flimsy dishtowel displayed the fact that it was starting to unravel, a little proud to be showing off how it was made — these things meant something. That they had been used and discarded and then rescued for future use; that women had worn those dresses and aprons, worn them out, meanwhile caring for them, washing, ironing, mending and finally choosing what deserved to be saved, added to their strange drama. I envied whoever had had charge of them and had gotten to know them intimately during their life cycle until they were faded and frayed. That person could understand their language.

Similarly, you are apt to bring together very unlikely things in your poems. In "Daffy Duck in Hollywood," you bring together cartoons, allusions to Parmigianino's painting, which was the inspiration for "Self Portrait in a Convex Mirror," the author as "that mean old cartoonist," various characters from literature, modern architecture ("New Brutalism"), and a whole series of unlikely items. As in this list near the beginning of the poem: "a mint-condition can of Rumford's Baking Powder, a celluloid earring, Speedy Gonzales, the latest from Helen Topping Miller's fertile escritoire, a sheaf of suggestive pix on greige, deckle-edged stock . . ."

JA [*as an aside*]: It should be Rumford, but I preferred the sound of Rumford's.

JY: I think of a collagist as someone who never throws anything out, and that your poems can be like that, that you can — if you wish — put anything and everything into a poem. Or, as you have also said, leave everything out.

JA: You mean the opening of my poem "The New Spirit": "I thought that if I could put it all down, that would be one way. And next the thought came to me that to leave all out would be another, and truer, way."

JY: In some ways, your Manhattan apartment and Hudson house are like the list in "Daffy Duck in Hollywood," full of all kinds of things next to each other.

JA: Yes, I'm firmly eclectic in these and in most things.

JY: When I studied with you at Brooklyn College in 1975, you were still making collages. I remember you once said, "You can make a collage on a postcard, and then write a poem based on it."

The first collage of yours I saw was *L'Heure Exquise* from 1977, which was first exhibited at the Drawing Center in New York City in November of that year. The next collage that was shown was in *Artifacts at the End of a Decade,* a collaborative artists' book with work by forty-four artists in a variety of media, which came out in 1981 and also included work by Laurie Anderson, R. Crumb, Sol Lewitt, Lucio Pozzi, Robert Kushner, and Robert Wilson. Starting in 1998, when you showed two collages from the early 1970s at Carrie Haddad Gallery in Hudson, New York, more attention began to be paid to this little-known side of you: your involvement with making visual art, rather than writing about it or collaborating with visual artists. Were you making collages during this period — say, from the mid 1970s until the late 1990s?

JA: I don't think I did very much. I mean, I didn't think anybody would ever be interested in them. I even kind of forgot about them myself, and then David and I were cleaning out stuff and came upon a shoebox full of my old postcards with my old collages mixed in. Somehow word got out, and Carrie Haddad asked if she could include a couple in a group show she was curating for her gallery in the late 1990s, and that show sparked wider interest in them. Trevor Winkfield and Brice Brown published a selection of them in the first issue of *The Sienese Shredder* in 2006, which led to an invitation to have my first solo show at Tibor de Nagy Gallery in New York in 2008, so I started making new ones for that show.

JY: When did you start making the bigger collages? I remember seeing a set of collages called "Chutes and Ladders" in that show at Tibor's.

CHUTES AND LADDERS I (FOR JOE BRAINARD), 2008 (14.5 x 19.5 in.)

CHUTES AND LADDERS II (FOR OLIVIER BROSSARD), 2008 (17.125 x 22.25 IN.)

JA: Not all of my early collages were postcards, of course, but I started making the big ones for my first show at Tibor's in 2008. There's one in that series that's dedicated to Joe Brainard. He used to mail me things that he'd cut out, with notes to use them in my collages. I actually thought that one had been lost, and was enormously relieved when I discovered that it's in a fine private collection in Connecticut. It's one of my first big collages.

JY: When did you meet Joe Brainard?

JA: I met him when I came back to New York in 1963. In those days I didn't fly, and it was hard to visit America because I could only get to New York by taking a ship. I was complaining to Jane [Freilicher] about missing New York, and she offered to pay for my ticket. It was in the summer when I sailed back. While I was here, Frank had a party for me at his loft on Broadway, across from Grace Church. I met Joe on the street outside — no, actually, I met Joe outside Kenward's apartment on Cornelia Street. Kenward was also giving a party for me. Joe was nervous and shy and pacing up and down the sidewalk. I also talked to him at the party. He was different from the others — bashful and innocent. I liked him immediately, and he certainly was not like anyone else at the party, which I found endearing.

JY: I see that you have a few board games lying around your house as well as plenty of art magazines. You're a bit of a pack rat, aren't you?

JA: Yes. I'd collect these vintage game boards, Chutes and Ladders, Chinese Checkers, Parcheesi, and others. David and other people would give them to me as Christmas and birthday presents. I'd have them reproduced from photographs my assistant took, and then use them as backgrounds for some of my bigger collages.

JY: You've been making collages for years now. How often do you create them these days?

JA: Whenever I think of one. We have a friend who works for us, dealing with parts of my archive and doing odd jobs, who comes to help me with the cutting and gluing, which I'm not too good at anymore. It depends on his hours a little bit. Usually, we work in the afternoon, and we make occasional trips to the Book Barn for source material. I go there for the old art catalogs, which they sell for, like, three dollars. And I'll bring those home and cut them up.

JY: Have you seen in person a lot of the art that you're cutting out?

JA: A lot of them are ones I haven't seen. They're from catalogs like Sotheby's or Christie's, rather than big art books. I always feel funny about cutting up an art book, although when I start to do it, I get carried away.

JY: In the recent collages, you seem much more gay than you've ever been in any of your work, don't you think?

JA: I beg your pardon? [*Laughter.*] No, I agree.

JY: I mean, I love the recent collage *To the City* (2016), the one of those two guys in little tennis whites, waiting to hitchhike — I thought, "That is so gay. Which one's John, and which one's David?" [*Laughter.*]

JA: I got that postcard at a cafe in Montpellier when I was a Fulbright student, in 1955 or something. I also had another postcard of two guys camping out, with one of them crouching down and holding a baguette in a suggestive position.

JY: They're much more gay than you've ever been in your written work. How interested were you in the visualization of gayness when you were a young man? Were you into campy stuff? Like drag queens from the 1950s? How involved with it were you?

JA: My lips are sealed. I mean, I knew about all that, but I chose not to write about it.

JY: But it seems all that campiness is now coming into your collages, in some way.

JA: My play, *The Heroes,* is really campy. That's from the early '50s. Very early '50s. I wrote that in January 1950.

JY: I'm trying to get at something, that you perhaps let your guard down, in a way, in the collages. Do you feel that it's different?

JA: I don't know. It just sort of bubbled up, from down below [*laughs*].

TO THE CITY, 2016 (11 x 8.5 in.)

JY: But there's also a lot from your childhood in these collages, too. I mean, you feel it with the *Krazy Kat* cartoon, and some of the other cartoon references. Are some of these collages autobiographical?

JA: Yeah, more or less. Like comic strips of my life, aside from *Krazy Kat.*

JY: In that regard, there's also this sense of innocence. That these images never descend into parody.

JA: You're absolutely right.

JY: And there are also all those images you get out of catalogs for men's wear — the images of the lower part of a man wearing pants, corduroys, for example. I was reminded of Robert Rauschenberg's sequence of photographs "Cy + Roman Steps" (1952), showing Cy Twombly descending the steps until the last photograph, which focuses on his crotch. The images that you choose aren't as direct, but there is an erotic charge to them.

JA: No comment.

JY: In a number of recent collages, you have the image of a strawberry. In one collage, there is a strawberry on a bed of nearly the same color, which you showed in your two-person show with Guy Maddin at Tibor de Nagy. And there is a strawberry in the collage *To the City.* Did you know that "strawberry" is slang for "someone who exchanges sex for drugs"?

JA: No.

JY: I remember once we were watching some movie, it was a film noir from the late 1940s or early '50s. It was a black-and-white movie, and you said, "That's actually what it was like back then." And I remember thinking, "What is he talking about? This is a weird New York City movie!" And you just up and said, "It was all in black-and-white." [*Laughter.*]

JA: Well, when I was growing up, we lived in the country, where it was difficult to go out and see movies, and I always had this sort of feeling that I was being deprived. And no matter how many I saw, I felt this hunger for films. And it's probably still with me.

JY: When I was looking at your collages, with their near and far perspectives, I thought, "Oh, that comes from seeing movies in the '50s, after CinemaScope was invented." In CinemaScope, you can show close-up views and panoramic distance shots at the same time. In some films, such as Alfred Hitchcock's *Rear Window* (1954), in which he used VistaVision, you see a fake backdrop; it's all constructed, and you just accept its artificiality. And I thought that this notion of the artificial was something in your work.

JA: Well, actually, de Chirico once wrote that a faked scene in a movie is much more real than the real thing would've been.

JY: In a way, your collages are like a scene from a movie that has never been made. It can combine a cartoon image with a photographic one of a landscape, which, of course, movies can do and have done. *Who Framed Roger Rabbit?* (1988), which you told me to go see, combines live-action and animation, for example. In a number of your recent collages, it's like you are about to undertake a journey or begin a dream.

JA: That's how I feel much of the time.

NOTRE DAME DES NEIGES, 1977 (7 x 5 IN.)

P.K., 2015 (10 x 8.25 in.)

ALICE, 2008 (3.5 x 5.5 in.)

"controls"

1.

    Here is everything for everyone

you gets a delicious picnic lunch

leathers . . . sleek fit . . . perspiration

a yellow straw profile

(made of a strong paper-like
substance)

Correspondence should be

        what Kleenex is to the
handkerchief

luminous lovelies that help to lighten that load.

                  A par-
ticularly interesting effect can be seen
if a solid tube is inserted in the
window through one of the openings.

2.

        Before his coming the city was
singularly devoted to the raucous,

3.

surrey to take you up into the mountains —

        a marvellous idea for travelling.

         buy packages of snap-in sections

        of a small room the inside of which is completely covered
with leaves.

                . . . tawny, tantalizing

Hoboken

(A collage made from Roget's Thesaurus)

Excitation, excitation of feeling,
Excitement, mental excitement,
Heart interest [slang], sensationalism,
Yellow journalism, melodrama, irritation,
Etc. (resentment) 900; passion, thrill, etc.
(State of excitability) 825.2–5.

Work *or* operate on *or* upon.
Stir, set astir, stir up, stir the blood.
Fillip, give a fillip.
Illumine.
Illuminate; fire, set on fire; inflame.
Apply the torch, fire, *or* warm the blood.
Fan, fan into a flame, fan the fire *or* flame.
Blow the coals, stir the embers, feed the fire, add fuel to the fire.

Change color, turn color,
Mantle; whiten, pale, turn pale; darken, turn black in the face, look black *or* blue;
Turn red, blush, flush, crimson, glow, warm.

Voice of the charmer, flattering tongue, unctuousness, mealymouthedness, etc.,
Humor, soothe, pet, coquet, slaver, beslaver, beslubber, beplaster, pat on the back, puff.
Fool to the top of one's bent.
Do one proud, pull one's leg, sawder, soft-sawder, soft-
Soap, butter, honey, jolly, blarney, lay
It on, lay it on thick [all coll.]; lay it
On with a trowel, string, string along,
Honeyfogle [U.S.], oil, soap [all slang];
Make things pleasant, gild the pill.

What is the use of running when you are
On the wrong road — J. Ray. *Mentis gratissimus error* — A most pleasant
　　apprehension. — Horace.
One goes to the right, the other to the left; both err, but in different ways. — Horace.
　　Who errs and mends, to God him-
Self commends. — Cervantes. To err is human, to forgive
Divine. — Pope. Errors is worse than ignorance. — P. J. Bailey.

Will-o'-the-wisp.

Off the track; on a false scent,
On the wrong scent *or*
Trail, up the wrong tree; at cross pur-
Poses.

Intense darkness, pitch-darkness, Cimmerian darkness,
Stygian darkness, Egyptian darkness, monte, reversi,
Squeezers, old maid, beggar-my-neighbor, goat, hearts, patience.

Dull, dullsome, dull as dish water.
"The face
That launched a thousand ships."
Wind-swept, bleak, raw, exposed,
The storm is up and all is on the hazard,
Rainy, showery, pluvious.

Avant-courier, *avant-coureur* or *avant courrier,*
Disentangle.
Vice-sultan, vice-caliph, vice-queen,
Bitter as gall.
Liqueur, cordial, sweet wine, punch,
Beanstalk.
"Leave not a rack behind."
All moonshine, all stuff and nonsense, all tommyrot,
"Thick as autumnal leaves that strow the brooks in Vallambrosa."
Bags, barrels, tons, flock,
In one's stead.
Prolocutrice *or* prolocutrix,
Accept the stewardship of the Chiltern hundreds.
View with disfavor, view with dark *or* jaundiced eyes,
Loblolly pine.
Ineptitude, inaptitude,
"As like as eggs,"
Swim *or* go with the stream.
Myrtle, turtledove, Cupid's bow,
Cupid's dart; love token etc. 902-5,
Bewitch, enrapture, inflame with love, carry away, turn the head.

Once in a blue moon [coll.],
Once in a coon's age [coll.],
Continually, incessantly, without ceasing, at all times, ever and anon;
Every day, every hour, every moment,
Daily, hourly, etc.
Daily and hourly, night and day, day and night, morning, noon and night,
Hour after hour, day after day, month after month, year after year,
Day in day out, month in month out, year in year out;
Perpetually, always etc. 112.5; invariably etc. 16.7.
Wander etc. from the truth,
Be in the wrong, be in the wrong box,
Bark up the wrong tree, back the wrong horse,
Aim at a pigeon and kill a crow,
Take *or* get the wrong sow by the ear,
The wrong pig by the tail, *or* the wrong bull by the horns,
Put the saddle on the wrong horse, count one's chickens before they are hatched,
Reckon without one's host, misbelieve, sin,
By special favor, yes, by all means.

I refuse! By no manner of means! I will not! Far be it from me!
Not if I can help it! I won't! Like fun I will!
Count me out! You have another guess coming! Catch me!

Volunteer, come forward, be a candidate,
Barkis is willin'.

Don't! Don't do that! Enough!
No more of that! That will never do! Leave off! Hands off!
Keep off! Keep off the grass! Hold! Stop! etc.
Refusal, refusing, declining, etc.

Leave alone, leave it to me,
Leave the door open, open the door to.
Open the floodgates, give the reins to etc. (allow freedom).

Above par.
Best, very best, choice, select.
Picked, elect, prime, capital, of the first water.
First-rate. First-class. First-chop.
Top-hole. Bang-up. Tiptop.

Top-notch. A 1, A one or number 1.
Crack, gilt-edge *or* gilt-edged.
Good, superb, super, superfine, exquisite,
High-wrought, precious, worth-its-weight-in-gold.

Worth a king's ransom,
Precious as the apple of the eye.

Good as gold,
Priceless, beyond price.

Invaluable, inestimable, rare.
Exceptional, extraordinary.

Beau idéal

Chevalier sans peur et sans reproche

Undeformed

Beyond all praise, *sans peur et sans reproche*

Clean, clean as a whistle, completely (etc.)

Koh-i-noor

Corker, trump [both slang]

Black tulip

Cygne noir, black swan

Admirable Crichton, Bayard, Roland, Sidney

Parasol.

Choice, best etc.

Standard, pattern, mirror etc. (prototype) 22

3:10 TO YUMA, 1972 (3.5 x 5.5 in.)

277.　　　　　　　　　　　　　INTERIOR, GARFIELD PARK CONSERVATORY, CHICAGO.

CONSERVATORY, CA. 1972 (3.5 x 5.5 IN.)

SIX O'CLOCK, 2008 (4.75 x 7 IN.)

Canzone

Until the first chill
No door sat on the clay.
When Billy brought on the chill
He began to chill.
No hand can
Point to the chill
It brought. Where a chill
Was, the grass grows.
Acts punish the chill
Showing summer in the grass.
The acts are grass.

Acts of our grass
Transporting chill
Over brazen grass
That retorts as grass
Leave the clay,
The grass,
And that which is grass.
The far formal forest can,
Used doubts can
Sit on the grass.
Hark! The sadness grows
In pain. The shadow grows.

All that grows
In deep shadow or grass
Is lifted to what grows.
Walking, a space grows.
Beyond, weeds chill
Toward night which grows.
Looking about, nothing grows.
Now a whiff of clay
Respecting clay
Or that which grows
Brings on what can.
And no one can.

The sprinkling can
Slumbered on the dock. Clay
Leaked from a can.
Normal heads can
Touch barbed-wire grass
If they can
Sing the old song of can
Waiting for a chill
In the chill
That without a can
Is painting less clay
Therapeutic colors of clay.

We got out into the clay
As a boy can.
Yet there's another kind of clay
Not arguing clay,
As time grows
Not getting larger, but mad clay
Looked for clay,
And grass
Begun seeming, grass
Struggling up out of clay
Into the first chill
To be quiet and raucous in the chill.

The chill
Flows over burning grass.
Not time grows.
So odd lights can
Fall on sinking clay.

THE GLEANERS, 1972 (3.5 x 5.5 in.)

BREEZEWAY, 2014 (9.25 x 7.5 in.)

"Tiepolo Macaron"
John Ashbery
Nov. 4 2015

TIEPOLO MACARON, 2015 (13.75 x 10.25 IN.)

STILL LIFE, 2016 (11 x 8.5 in.)

Pantoum

Eyes shining without mystery,
Footprints eager for the past
Through the vague snow of many clay pipes,
And what is in store?

Footprints eager for the past
The usual obtuse blanket.
And what is in store
For those dearest to the king?

The usual obtuse blanket.
Of legless regrets and amplifications
For those dearest to the king.
Yes, sirs, connoisseurs of oblivion,

The usual obtuse blanket.
Of legless regrets and amplifications
For those dearest to the king.
Yes, sirs, connoisseurs of oblivion,

Of legless regrets and amplifications,
That is why a watchdog is shy.
Yes, sirs, connoisseurs of oblivion,
These days are short, brittle; there is only one night.

That is why a watchdog is shy,
Why the court, trapped in a silver storm, is dying.
These days are short, brittle; there is only one night
And that soon gotten over.

Why the court, trapped in a silver storm, is dying
Some blunt pretense to safety we have
And that soon gotten over
For they must have motion.

Some blunt pretense to safety we have
Eyes shining without mystery,
For they must have motion
Through the vague snow of many clay pipes.

ACROBATS, CA. 1972 (3.5 x 5.5 IN.)

MOTOR COURT, 2010 (4.25 x 5.5 in.)

A DREAM OF HEROES, 2015 (15.75 x 20.5 in.)

"The Painter" John Ashbery 2014

THE PAINTER, 2014 (15 x 20.5 in.)

The Painter

Sitting between the sea and the buildings
He enjoyed painting the sea's portrait.
But just as children imagine a prayer
Is merely silence, he expected his subject
To rush up the sand, and, seizing a brush,
Plaster its own portrait on the canvas.

So there was never any paint on his canvas
Until the people who lived in the buildings
Put him to work: "Try using the brush
As a means to an end. Select, for a portrait,
Something less angry and large, and more subject
To a painter's moods, or, perhaps, to a prayer."

How could he explain to them his prayer
That nature, not art, might usurp the canvas?
He chose his wife for a new subject,
Making her vast, like ruined buildings,
As if, forgetting itself, the portrait
Had expressed itself without a brush.

Slightly encouraged, he dipped his brush
In the sea, murmuring a heartfelt prayer:
"My soul, when I paint this next portrait
Let it be you who wrecks the canvas."
The news spread like wildfire through the buildings:
He had gone back to the sea for his subject.

Imagine a painter crucified by his subject!
Too exhausted even to lift his brush,
He provoked some artists leaning from the buildings
To malicious mirth: "We haven't a prayer
Now, of putting ourselves on canvas,
Or getting the sea to sit for a portrait!"

Others declared it a self-portrait.
Finally all indications of a subject
Began to fade, leaving the canvas

Perfectly white. He put down the brush.
At once a howl, that was also a prayer,
Arose from the overcrowded buildings.

They tossed him, the portrait, from the tallest of the buildings;
And the sea devoured the canvas and the brush
As though his subject had decided to remain a prayer.

MANNERIST CONCERNS, 2008 (16.475 x 16.5 in.)

He

He cuts down the lakes so they appear straight
He smiles at his feet in their tired mules.
He turns up the music much louder.
He takes down the vaseline from the pantry shelf.

He is the capricious smile behind colored bottles.
He eats not lest the poor want some.
He breathes of attitudes the piney altitudes.
He indeed is the White Cliffs of Dover.

He knows that his neck is frozen.
He snorts in the vale of dim wolves.
He writes to say, "If ever you visit this island,
He'll grow you back to your childhood.

"He is the liar behind the hedge
He grew one morning out of candor.
He is his own consolation prize.
He has had his eye on you from the beginning."

He hears the weak cut down with a smile.
He waltzes tragically on the spitting housetops.
He is never near. What you need
He cancels with the air of one making a salad.

He is always the last to know.
He is strength you once said was your bonnet.
He has appeared in "Carmen."
He is after us. If you decide

He is important, it will get you nowhere.
He is the source of much bitter reflection.
He used to be pretty for a rat.
He is now over-proud of his Etruscan appearance.

He walks in his sleep into your life.
He is worth knowing only for the children
He has reared as savages in Utah.
He helps his mother take in the clothes-line.

He is unforgettable as a shooting star.
He is known as "Liverlips."
He will tell you he has had a bad time of it.
He will try to pretend his pressagent is a temptress.

He looks terrible on the stairs.
He cuts himself on what he eats.
He was last seen flying to New York.
He was handing out cards which read:

"He wears a question in his left eye.
He dislikes the police but will associate with them.
He will demand something not on the menu.
He is invisible to the eyes of beauty and culture.

"He prevented the murder of Mistinguett in Mexico.
He has a knack for abortions. If you see
He is following you, forget him immediately:
He is dangerous even though asleep and unarmed."

FIT OF PEAK, 2008 (4.125 x 5.875 in.)

DIFFUSION OF KNOWLEDGE, CA. 1972 (3.5 x 5.5 IN.)

GOTCHA!, 1972 (3.5 x 5.5 in.)

BINGO BEETHOVEN, 2014 (8.25 x 7.5 in.)

from **Europe**

1.
To employ her
construction ball
Morning fed on the
light blue wood
of the mouth
                cannot understand
feels deeply)

2.
A wave of nausea —
numerals

3.
a few berries

4.
the unseen claw
Babe asked today
The background poles roped over
into star jolted them

5.
filthy or into backward drenched flung heaviness
lemons asleep pattern crying

6.
The month of elephant —
embroidery over where
ill page sees.

7.
What might have
   children singing
the horses
            the seven
breaths under tree, fog
clasped — absolute, unthinking
menace to our way of life.
uh unearth more cloth
This could have been done —
This could not be done

8.
In the falling twilight of the wintry afternoon all looked dull and cheerless. The car stood
outside with Ronald Pryor and Collins attending to some slight engine trouble — the
fast, open car which Ronnie sometimes used to such advantage. It was covered with mud,
after the long run from Suffolk, for they had started from Harbury long before daylight,
and, until an hour ago, had been moving swiftly up the Great North Road, by way of
Stanford, Grantham and Doncaster to York. There they had turned away to Ripon,
where, for an hour, they had eaten and rested. In a basket the waiter had placed some cold
food with some bread and a bottle of wine, and this had been duly transferred to the car.

All was now ready for the continuance of the journey.

9.
The decision in his life
soul elsewhere
the gray hills
out there on the road darkness
covering lieutenant

   there is a cure

10.
He had mistaken his book for garbage. [. . .]

PROMENADE, 2011 (8.25 x 8.125 IN.)

PARK, 2010 (11 x 8.5 in.)

from **Idaho**

I.

During the past few months, Biff had become quite a frequent visitor to Carol's apartment.

He never failed to marvel at the cool, corrected elegance of the place as contrasted with its warm, rippling, honey-blonde occupant. The apothecary jars,

Chippendale furniture,

and wall-to-wall

carpeting were strangely out of keeping with Carol's habitual "Hiya good lookin'" as she came forward to greet him, wrapped in one of those big fuzzy bathrobes and drying her hair on a Turkish towel. Or were his calculations somehow awry? Was there, deep within this warm, vital-seeming presence a steel vein so thin as to be almost invisible? Or was this, too, a mistake?

Their whole conduct had been, up to now, not impersonal exactly, but utterly devoid of any recognition of sex-consciousness. In conversation they had "swapped backgrounds," as Biff called it. Carol, her eyes wet with tears at the picture of his isolation in the crowded rectory, had uttered a deep sigh at her own recital of being left for the first eight years of her life to the sole care of Patches.

With the unconscious dramatic heightening that always goes with a sympathetic audience, each of them, intensely serious and really moved, had lifted corners of the veil for the other to peep through. They had been very close to each other in attention, in sympathy, in response, but with none of the subtle emphasis which marks the recognized intrusion of sex. Carol was aware today, however, that Biff had suddenly become obsessed with a sense of her; that he had caught fire.

She was aware of

vast excitement,

apprehension,

a mental

"Can I give you a hand?"
She gave a little cry that was silenced by mouth on
uttermost tingling nerve
"Carol!" he said. Can this be the one time
???

She had known how from

Biff: The last Rhode Island reds are
"diet of hamburgers and orange juice"
Exactly what kind of perfection??

73

I see into fields of timothy,
                             one
the others   time
                        change
,,,,,,and they walked back,
                   small hand-assemblies

                         "What does it mean?????????????
                         Carol laughed. Among other things,
                              till I've finished it. It's the reason of
                         dropped into Brentano's.
                                        get some of the
                         a pile of these. I just grabbed one . . .
                                   — Oh, by the way, there's a tele-
                         "See?" She pointed to the table.
Cornelia unfolded the piece of crude blue paper that is a
         French telegra.
                   # # # # # # # # # # # # # #
                              The mouth of weeds

                    marriage." She shivered. It's — it's a death!" [. . .]

THE LEISURE CLASS, 2011 (12 × 14 in.)

FOUNTAIN, 2010 (5.75 x 3.5 IN.)

Farm Implements and Rutabagas in a Landscape

The first of the undecoded messages read: "Popeye sits in thunder,
Unthought of. From that shoebox of an apartment,
From livid curtain's hue, a tangram emerges: a country."
Meanwhile the Sea Hag was relaxing on a green couch: "How pleasant
To spend one's vacation *en la casa de Popeye,*" she scratched
Her cleft chin's solitary hair. She remembered spinach

And was going to ask Wimpy if he had bought any spinach.
"M'love," he intercepted, "the plains are decked out in thunder
Today, and it shall be as you wish." He scratched
The part of his head under his hat. The apartment
Seemed to grow smaller. "But what if no pleasant
Inspiration plunge us now to the stars? *For this is my country*."

Suddenly they remembered how it was cheaper in the country.
Wimpy was thoughtfully cutting open a number 2 can of spinach
When the door opened and Swee'pea crept in. "How pleasant!"
But Swee'pea looked morose. A note was pinned to his bib. "Thunder
And tears are unavailing," it read. "Henceforth shall Popeye's apartment
Be but remembered space, toxic or salubrious, whole or scratched."

Olive came hurtling through the window; its geraniums scratched
Her long thigh. "I have news!" she gasped. "Popeye, forced as you know to flee the country
One musty gusty evening, by the schemes of his wizened, duplicate father, jealous of
    the apartment
And all that it contains, myself and spinach
In particular, heaves bolts of loving thunder
At his own astonished becoming, rupturing the pleasant

Arpeggio of our years. No more shall pleasant
Rays of the sun refresh your sense of growing old, nor the scratched
Tree-trunks and mossy foliage, only immaculate darkness and thunder."
She grabbed Swee'pea. "I'm taking the brat to the country."
"But you can't do that — he hasn't even finished his spinach,"
Urged the Sea Hag, looking fearfully around at the apartment.

But Olive was already out of earshot. Now the apartment
Succumbed to a strange new hush. "Actually it's quite pleasant
Here," thought the Sea Hag. "If this is all we need fear from spinach
Then I don't mind so much. Perhaps we could invite Alice the Goon over" —
    she scratched
One dug pensively — "but Wimpy is such a country
Bumpkin, always burping like that." Minute at first, the thunder

Soon filled the apartment. It was domestic thunder,
The color of spinach. Popeye chuckled and scratched
His balls: it sure was pleasant to spend a day in the country.

VALABRE — Le Château du Roi René

CHATEAU, CA. 1972 (3.5 x 5.5 IN.)

CORONA, 2011 (16.5 x 16.5 in.)

from **Daffy Duck in Hollywood**

Something strange is creeping across me.
La Celestina has only to warble the first few bars
Of "I Thought about You" or something mellow from
Amadigi di Gaula for everything — a mint-condition can
Of Rumford's Baking Powder, a celluloid earring, Speedy
Gonzales, the latest from Helen Topping Miller's fertile
Escritoire, a sheaf of suggestive pix on greige, deckle-edged
Stock — to come clattering through the rainbow trellis
Where Pistachio Avenue rams the 2300 block of Highland
Fling Terrace. He promised he'd get me out of this one,
That mean old cartoonist, but just look what he's
Done to me now! I scarce dare approach me mug's attenuated
Reflection in yon hubcap, so jaundiced, so *déconfit*
Are its lineaments — fun, no doubt, for some quack phrenologist's
Fern-clogged waiting room, but hardly what you'd call
Companionable. But everything is getting choked to the point of
Silence. Just now a magnetic storm hung in the swatch of sky
Over the Fudds' garage, reducing it — drastically —
To the aura of a plumbago-blue log cabin on
A Gadsden Purchase commemorative cover. Suddenly all is
Loathing. I don't want to go back inside any more. You meet
Enough vague people on this emerald traffic-island — no,
Not people, comings and goings, more: mutterings, splatterings,
The bizarrely but effectively equipped infantries of happy-go-nutty
Vegetal jacqueries, plumed, pointed at the little
White cardboard castle over the mill run. "Up
The lazy river, how happy we could be?"
How will it end? That geranium glow
Over Anaheim's had the riot act read to it by the
Etna-size firecracker that exploded last minute into
A *carte du Tendre* in whose lower right-hand corner
(Hard by the jock-itch sand-trap that skirts
The asparagus patch of algolagnic *nuits blanches*) Amadis
Is cozening the Princesse de Cleves into a midnight micturition spree
On the Tamigi with the Wallets (Walt, Blossom, and little
Sleezix) on a lamé barge "borrowed" from Ollie
Of the Movies' dread mistress of the robes. Wait!
I have an announcement! This wide, tepidly meandering,
Civilized Lethe (one can barely make out the maypoles

And *châlets de nécessité* on its sedgy shore) leads to Tophet, that
Landfill-haunted, not-so-residential resort from which
Some travellers return! This whole moment is the groin
Of a borborygmic giant who even now
Is rolling over on us in his sleep. Farewell bocages,
Tanneries, water-meadows. The allegory comes unsnarled
Too soon; a shower of pecky acajou harpoons is
About all there is to be noted between tornadoes. I have
Only my intermittent life in your thoughts to live
Which is like thinking in another language. Everything
Depends on whether somebody reminds you of me.
That this is a fabulation, and that those "other times"
Are in fact the silences of the soul, picked out in
Diamonds on stygian velvet, matters less than it should.
Prodigies of timing may be arranged to convince them
We live in one dimension, they in ours. While I
Abroad through all the coasts of dark destruction seek
Deliverance for us all, think in that language: its
Grammar, though tortured, offers pavilions
At each new parting of the ways. Pastel
Ambulances scoop up the quick and hie them to hospitals.
"It's all bits and pieces, spangles, patches, really; nothing
Stands alone. What happened to creative evolution?"
Sighed Aglavaine. Then to her Sélysette: "If his
Achievement is only to end up less boring than the others,
What's keeping us here? Why not leave at once?
I have to stay here while they sit in there,
Laugh, drink, have fine time. In my day
One lay under the tough green leaves,
Pretending not to notice how they bled into
The sky's aqua, the wafted-away no-color of regions supposed
Not to concern us. And so we too
Came where the others came: nights of physical endurance,
Or if, by day, our behavior was anarchically
Correct, at least by New Brutalism standards, all then
Grew taciturn by previous agreement. We were spirited
Away *en bateau,* under cover of fudge dark. [. . .]

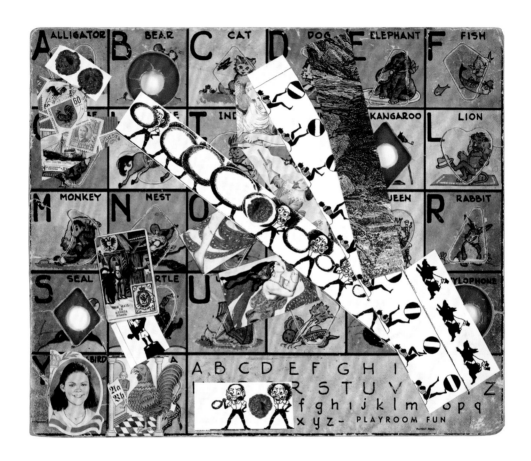

THE MAIL IN RUSSIA, 2011 (13 X 15.5 IN.)

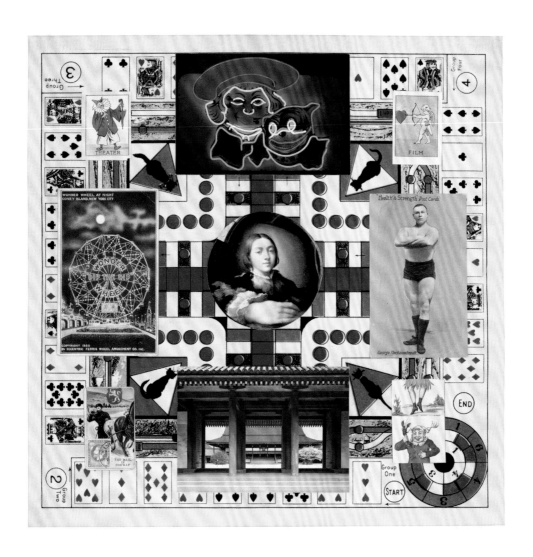

THE MAIL IN NORWAY, 2009 (16.25 x 16.25 in.)

THE "LITTLE" TOWER OF BABEL, 2010 (6.75 x 8.25 in.)

HELLO HAZEL, CA. 1972 (5.5 x 3.5 IN.)

from **The Songs We Know Best**

Just like a shadow in an empty room
Like a breeze that's pointed from beyond the tomb
Just like a project of which no one tells —
Or didja really think that I was somebody else?

Your clothes and pantlegs lookin' out of shape
Shape of the body over which they drape
Body which has acted in so many scenes
But didja ever think of what that body means?

It is an organ and a vice to some
A necessary evil which we all must shun
To others an abstraction and a piece of meat
But when you're looking out you're in the driver's seat!

No man cares little about fleshly things
They fill him with a silence that spreads in rings
We wish to know more but we are never sated
No wonder some folks think the flesh is overrated!

The things we know now all got learned in school
Try to learn a new thing and you break the rule
Our knowledge isn't much it's just a small amount
But you feel it quick inside you when you're down for the count

You look at me and frown like I was out of place
I guess I never did much for the human race
Just hatched some schemes on paper that looked good at first
Sat around and watched until the bubble burst

And now you're lookin' good all up and down the line
Except for one thing you still have in mind
It's always there though often with a different face
It's the worm inside the jumping bean that makes it race [. . .]

PIE IN THE SKY, 2016 (11 x 8.75 IN.)

ROYAL FAMILY II, 2014 (11 x 8.5 in.)

HOTEL NEGRESCO, 2010 (6.25 x 5.5 in.)

37 Haiku

Old-fashioned shadows hanging down, that difficulty in love too soon

Some star or other went out, and you, thank you for your book and year

Something happened in the garage and I owe it for the blood traffic

Too low for nettles but it is exactly the way people think and feel

And I think there's going to be even more but waist-high

Night occurs dimmer each time with the pieces of light smaller and squarer

You have original artworks hanging on the walls oh I said edit

You nearly undermined the brush I now place against the ball field arguing

That love was a round place and will still be there two years from now

And it is a dream sailing in a dark unprotected cove

Pirates imitate the ways of ordinary people myself for instance

Planted over and over that land has a bitter aftertaste

A blue anchor grains of grit in a tall sky sewing

He is a monster like everyone else but what do you do if you're a monster

Like him feeling him come from far away and then go down to his car

The wedding was enchanted everyone was glad to be in it

What trees, tools, why ponder socks on the premises

Come to the edge of the barn the property really begins there

In a smaller tower shuttered and put away there

You lay aside your hair like a book that is too important to read now

Why did witches pursue the beast from the eight sides of the country

A pencil on glass — shattered! The water runs down the drain

In winter sometimes you see those things and also in summer

A child must go down it must stand and last

Too late the last express passes through the dust of gardens

A vest — there is so much to tell about even in the side rooms

Hesitantly, it built up and passed quickly without unlocking

There are some places kept from the others and are separate, they never exist

I lost my ridiculous accent without acquiring another

In Buffalo, Buffalo she was praying, the nights stick together like pages in an old book

The dreams descend like cranes on gilded, forgetful wings

What is the past, what is it all for? A mental sandwich?

Did you say, hearing the schooner overhead, we turned back to the weir?

In rags and crystals, sometimes with a shred of sense, an odd dignity

The box must have known the particles fell through the house after him

All in all we were taking our time, the sea returned — no more pirates

I inch and only sometimes as far as the twisted pole gone in spare color

CHUTES AND LADDERS III (FOR DAVID KERMANI), 2008 (18.5 x 18.375 IN.)

SPRING, CA. 1972 (5.5 x 3.5 IN.)

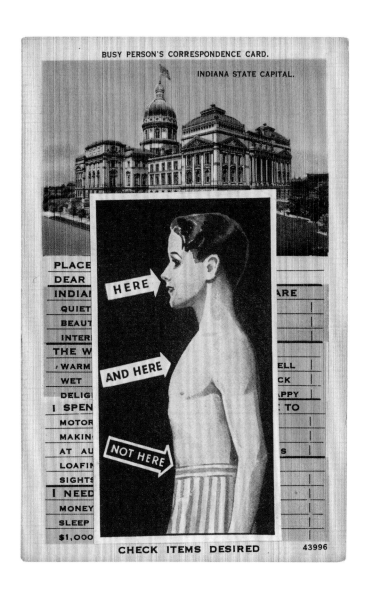

"WARM WET DELIGHT," CA. 1972 (5.5 x 3.5 IN.)

Finnish Rhapsody

He managed the shower, coped with the small spattering drops,
Then rubbed himself dry with a towel, wiped the living organism.
Day extended its long promise, light swept through his refuge.
But it was time for business, back to the old routine.

Many there are, a crowd exists at present,
For whom the daily forgetting, to whom the diurnal plunge
Truncates the spadelike shadows, chops off the blades of darkness,
To be rescued, to be guided into a state of something like security.
Yet it falls off for others; for some, however, it drops from sight:
The millers, winnowers of wheat,
Dusted with snow-white flour, glazed with farinaceous powder,
Like Pierrot, like the white clown of chamber music;
The leggy mannequins, models slender and tall;
The sad children, the disappointed kids.

And for these few, to this small group
Forgetting means remembering the ranks, oblivion is recalling the rows
Of flowers each autumn and spring; of blooms in the fall and early summer.
But those traveling by car, those nosing the vehicle out into the crowded highway
And at the posts of evening, the tall poles of declining day,
Returning satisfied, their objective accomplished,
Note neither mystery nor alarm, see no strangeness or cause for fright.
And these run the greatest risk at work, are endangered by their employment
Seeing there can be no rewards later, no guerdon save in the present:
Strong and severe punishment, *peine forte et dure*,
Or comfort and relaxation, coziness and tranquillity.

Don't fix it if it works, tinker not with that which runs apace,
Otherwise the wind might get it, the breeze waft it away.
There is no time for anything like chance, no spare moment for the aleatory,
Because the closing of our day is business, the bottom line already here.
One wonders what roadblocks we're set up for, we question barricades:
Is it better to time, jot down the performance time of
Anything irregular, all that doesn't fit the preconceived mold
Of our tentative offerings and withdrawals, our hesitant giving and taking back?
For those who perform correctly, for the accurate, painstaking ones
Do accomplish their business, get the job done,
And are seldom seen again, and are rarely glimpsed after that.

That there are a few more black carriages, more somber chariots
For some minutes, over a brief period,
Signifies business as usual, means everything is OK,
That the careful have gone to their reward, the capable disappeared
And boobies, or nincompoops, numskulls and sapheads,
Persist, faced with eventual destruction; endure to be confronted with annihilation
     someday.

The one who runs little, he who barely trips along
Knows how short the day is, how few the hours of light.
Distractions can't wrench him, preoccupations forcibly remove him
From the heap of things, the pile of this and that:
Tepid dreams and mostly worthless; lukewarm fancies, the majority of them unprofitable.
Yet it is from these that the light, from the ones present here that luminosity
Sifts and breaks, subsides and falls asunder.
And it will be but half-strange, really be only semi-bizarre
When the tall poems of the world, the towering earthbound poetic utterances
Invade the street of our dialect, penetrate the avenue of our patois,
Bringing fresh power and new knowledge, transporting virgin might and up-to-date
     enlightenment
To this place of honest thirst, to this satisfyingly parched here and now,
Since all things congregate, because everything assembles
In front of him, before the one
Who need only sit and tie his shoelace, who should remain seated, knotting the metal-
     tipped cord
For it to happen right, to enable it to come correctly into being
As moments, then years; minutes, afterwards ages
Suck up the common strength, absorb the everyday power
And afterwards live on, satisfied; persist, later to be a source of gratification,
But perhaps only to oneself, haply to one's sole identity.

©16049—MORNING GLORY POOL, YELLOWSTONE NATIONAL PARK

COPYRIGHT BY HAYNES STUDIOS INC., BOZEMAN, MONTANA

4A-H281

ICARUS, 2010 (3.5 x 5.5 IN.)

Wishing Well, Ramona's Marriage Place, San Diego, Cal.

OLD TOWN, CA. 1972 (3.5 x 5.5 IN.)

RESEARCH STUDIO, CA. 1972 (5.5 x 3.5 in.)

Hotel Lautréamont

1.
Research has shown that ballads were produced by all of society
working as a team. They didn't just happen. There was no guesswork.
The people, then, knew what they wanted and how to get it.
We see the results in works as diverse as "Windsor Forest" and "The Wife of Usher's Well."

Working as a team, they didn't just happen. There was no guesswork.
The horns of elfland swing past, and in a few seconds
we see the results in works as diverse as "Windsor Forest" and "The Wife of Usher's Well,"
or, on a more modern note, in the finale of the Sibelius violin concerto.

The horns of elfland swing past, and in a few seconds
the world, as we know it, sinks into dementia, proving narrative passé,
or in the finale of the Sibelius violin concerto.
Not to worry, many hands are making work light again.

The world, as we know it, sinks into dementia, proving narrative passé.
In any case the ruling was long overdue.
Not to worry, many hands are making work light again,
so we stay indoors. The quest was only another adventure.

2.
In any case, the ruling was long overdue.
The people are beside themselves with rapture
so we stay indoors. The quest was only another adventure
and the solution problematic, at any rate far off in the future.

The people are beside themselves with rapture
yet no one thinks to question the source of so much collective euphoria,
and the solution: problematic, at any rate far off in the future.
The saxophone wails, the martini glass is drained.

Yet no one thinks to question the source of so much collective euphoria.
In troubled times one looked to the shaman or priest for comfort and counsel.
The saxophone wails, the martini glass is drained,
and night like black swansdown settles on the city.

In troubled times one looked to the shaman or priest for comfort and counsel.
Now, only the willing are fated to receive death as a reward,
and night like black swansdown settles on the city.
If we tried to leave, would being naked help us?

3.
Now, only the willing are fated to receive death as a reward.
Children twist hula-hoops, imagining a door to the outside.
If we tried to leave, would being naked help us?
And what of older, lighter concerns? What of the river?

Children twist hula-hoops, imagining a door to the outside,
when all we think of is how much we can carry with us.
And what of older, lighter concerns? What of the river?
All the behemoths have filed through the maze of time.

When all we think of is how much we can carry with us
small wonder that those at home sit, nervous, by the unlit grate.
All the behemoths have filed through the maze of time.
It remains for us to come to terms with our commonality.

Small wonder that those at home sit nervous by the unlit grate.
It was their choice, after all, that spurred us to feats of the imagination.
It remains for us to come to terms with our commonality
and in so doing deprive time of further hostages.

4.
It was their choice, after all, that spurred us to feats of the imagination.
Now, silently as one mounts a stair we emerge into the open
and in so doing deprive time of further hostages,
to end the standoff that history long ago began.

Now, silently as one mounts a stair we emerge into the open
but it is shrouded, veiled: We must have made some ghastly error.
To end the standoff that history long ago began
must we thrust ever onward, into perversity?

But it is shrouded, veiled: We must have made some ghastly error.
You mop your forehead with a rose, recommending its thorns.
Must we thrust ever onward, into perversity?
Only night knows for sure; the secret is safe with her.

You mop your forehead with a rose, recommending its thorns.
Research has shown that ballads were produced by all of society;
only night knows for sure. The secret is safe with her:
The people, then, knew what they wanted and how to get it.

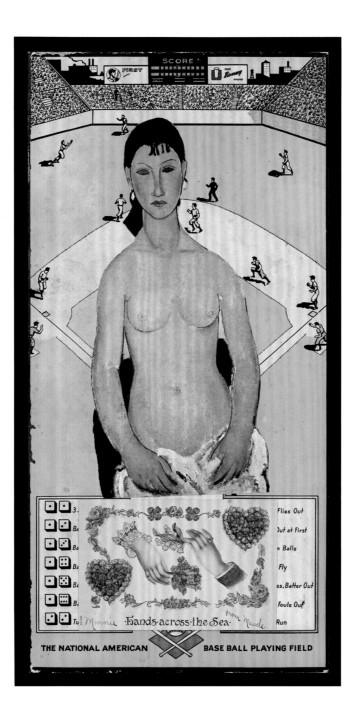

MINNIE FROM MAUDE, 2014 (17.25 x 9 in.)

14   A. Garcelon

TO GREET YOU, 2014 (12 x 9.25 in.)

from . . . **by an Earthquake**

A hears by chance a familiar name, and the name involves a riddle of the past.

B, in love with A, receives an unsigned letter in which the writer states that she is the mistress of A and begs B not to take him away from her.

B, compelled by circumstances to be a companion of A in an isolated place, alters her rosy views of love and marriage when she discovers, through A, the selfishness of men.

A, an intruder in a strange house, is discovered; he flees through the nearest door into a windowless closet and is trapped by a spring lock.

A is so content with what he has that any impulse toward enterprise is throttled.

A solves an important mystery when falling plaster reveals the place where some old love letters are concealed.

A-4, missing food from his larder, half believes it was taken by a "ghost."

A, a crook, seeks unlawful gain by selling A-8 an object, X, which A-8 already owns.

A sees a stranger, A-5, stealthily remove papers, X, from the pocket

of another stranger, A-8, who is asleep. A follows A-5.

A sends an infernal machine, X, to his enemy, A-3, and it falls into

the hands of A's friend, A-2.

Angela tells Philip of her husband's enlarged prostate, and asks for money.

Philip, ignorant of her request, has the money placed in an escrow account.

A discovers that his pal, W, is a girl masquerading as a boy.

A, discovering that W is a girl masquerading as a boy, keeps the knowledge to himself and does his utmost to save the masquerader from annoying experiences.

A, giving ten years of his life to a miserly uncle, U, in exchange for a college education, loses his ambition and enterprise.

A, undergoing a strange experience among a people weirdly deluded, discovers the secret of the delusion from Herschel, one of the victims who has died. By means of information obtained from the notebook, A succeeds in rescuing the other victims of the delusion.

A dies of psychic shock.

Albert has a dream, or an unusual experience, psychic or otherwise, which enables him to conquer a serious character weakness and become successful in his new narrative, "Boris Karloff."

Silver coins from the Mojave Desert turn up in the possession of a sinister jeweler.

Three musicians wager that one will win the affections of the local kapellmeister's wife; the losers must drown themselves in a nearby stream.

Ardis, caught in a trap and held powerless under a huge burning glass, is saved by an eclipse of the sun.

Kent has a dream so vivid that it seems a part of his waking experience.

A and A-2 meet with a tragic adventure, and A-2 is killed.

Elvira, seeking to unravel the mystery of a strange house in the hills, is caught in an electrical storm. During the storm the house vanishes and the site on which it stood becomes a lake.

Alphonse has a wound, a terrible psychic wound, an invisible psychic wound, which causes pain in flesh and tissue which, otherwise, are perfectly healthy and normal.

A has a dream which he conceives to be an actual experience.

Jenny, homeward bound, drives and drives, and is still driving, no nearer to her home than she was when she first started.

Petronius B. Furlong's friend, Morgan Windhover, receives a wound from which he dies.

Thirteen guests, unknown to one another, gather in a spooky house to hear Toe reading Buster's will.

Buster has left everything to Lydia, a beautiful Siamese girl poet of whom no one has heard.

Lassie and Rex tussle together politely; Lassie, wounded, is forced to limp home.

In the Mexican gold rush a city planner is found imprisoned by outlaws in a crude cage of sticks.

More people flow over the dam and more is learned about the missing electric cactus.

Too many passengers have piled onto a cable car in San Francisco; the conductor is obliged to push some of them off.

Maddalena, because of certain revelations she has received, firmly resolves that she will not carry out an enterprise that had formerly been dear to her heart. [. . .]

FAMILY, 2011 (16.25 x 13.25 in.)

POISSON D'AVRIL, CA. 1972 (5.5 x 3.5 IN.)

L'HEURE EXQUISE, 1977 (3.5 x 5.5 in.)

LA FÊTE À NEU-NEU, 2008 (4 x 6 in.)

The Dong with the Luminous Nose

(A cento)

Within a windowed niche of that high hall
I wake and feel the fell of dark, not day.
I shall rush out as I am, and walk the street
The lights begin to twinkle from the rocks
From camp to camp, through the foul womb of night.
Come, Shepherd, and again renew the quest.
And birds sit brooding in the snow.

Continuous as the stars that shine,
When all men were asleep the snow came flying
Near where the dirty Thames does flow
Through caverns measureless to man,
Where thou shalt see the red-gilled fishes leap
And a lovely Monkey with lollipop paws
Where the remote Bermudas ride.

Softly, in the dusk, a woman is singing to me:
This is the cock that crowed in the morn.
Who'll be the parson?
Beppo! That beard of yours becomes you not!
A gentle answer did the old Man make:
Farewell, ungrateful traitor,
Bright as a seedsman's packet
Where the quiet-coloured end of evening smiles.

Obscurest night involved the sky
And brickdust Moll had screamed through half a street:
"Look in my face; my name is Might-have-been,
Sylvan historian, who canst thus express
Every night and alle,
The happy highways where I went
To the hills of Chankly Bore!"

Where are you going to, my pretty maid?
These lovers fled away into the storm
And it's O dear, what can the matter be?
For the wind is in the palm-trees, and the temple bells they say:

Lay your sleeping head, my love,
On the wide level of the mountain's head,
Thoughtless as monarch oaks, that shade the plain,
In autumn, on the skirts of Bagley Wood.
A ship is floating in the harbour now,
Heavy as frost, and deep almost as life!

NORGE, CA. 1972 (3.5 x 5.5 IN.)

STRAWBERRY BED, 2015 (3.5 x 5.5 IN.)

APRÈS UN RÊVE, CA. 1977 (6.625 x 4.25 IN.)

They Knew What They Wanted

They all kissed the bride.
They all laughed.
They came from beyond space.
They came by night.

They came to a city.
They came to blow up America.
They came to rob Las Vegas.
They dare not love.

They died with their boots on.
They shoot horses, don't they?
They go boom.
They got me covered.

They flew alone.
They gave him a gun.
They just had to get married.
They live. They loved life.

They live by night.
They drive by night.
They knew Mr Knight.
They were expendable.

They met in Argentina.
They met in Bombay.
They met in the dark.
They might be giants.

They made me a fugitive.
They made me a criminal.
They only kill their masters.
They shall have music.

They were sisters.
They still call me Bruce.
They won't believe me.
They won't forget.

CIRCLE PARK, DEERINGS OAKS, PORTLAND, MAINE

5A-H2364

CIRCLE PARK, CA. 1972 (3.5 x 5.5 IN.)

TEMPLO EXPIATORIO, CA. 1972 (3.5 x 5.5 IN.)

MOON GLOW, 2008 (16 x 16.25 in.)

Haunted Ride

Yes, but . . . isn't that the point?
White house, you're not even seein'.
I'll take a rain check on the trees.
They've remembered.
                        Get the new attendant.
Ride the pink palomino. Like any big artist's leg
he wasn't rapturous,
                        only captivated.
Misguided police draped in cheerful Macbeth plaid
remembered never to toll the dying

brilliance of that great ball again,
the lava farm,
th' intrusive handle.

PROMONTORY, 2010 (13 x 7.75 in.)

Impermeable

Finally, alone.
I was asked, are you sure?
Then the spotlight took over, mended
degenerate fences, fixed frost.

Remember, keep things brash,
unprogrammed. Start the dormition
theory an inch above my head.

We'll never have to respond.
Renewal costs said, in a statement:
You don't need to survive.
Just existing would be enough.

Put his legs under it. Put
pants back on, towel and visitor.
Ladle thy grief in Japanese pinstripes.

Hopefully, northern nuances will be spared
this time around. A few of us sitting around
Rick and Amy's, were up half the night
examining selvage, or salvage.

NORTHERN LIGHTS, 2008 (12 x 9 in.)

NEMO, 2009 (12.25 x 9 in.)

CREDITS AND ACKNOWLEDGMENTS

All collages courtesy of the Tibor de Nagy Gallery, New York, except:

Harvard Advocate cover (Nov. 1948) by John Ashbery and Fred Amory. Courtesy of *The Harvard Advocate*.

Except as otherwise noted, all poems are reprinted by arrangement with Georges Borchardt, Inc., for the author.

The collage-poem "'controls'" (1952) was first published in *The Songs We Know Best: John Ashbery's Early Life* by Karin Roffman (New York: Farrar, Straus & Giroux, 2017). Copyright © 2017 by John Ashbery. All rights reserved.

"Hoboken" was first published in *Semi-Colon* (Vol. I, No. 3, undated [ca. 1953]); reprinted in *C: A Journal of Poetry* (Vol. I, No. 10, 1965); first collected in book form in John Ashbery, *Collected Poems 1991–2000* (New York: The Library of America, 2017).

"Canzone," "He," "Pantoum," and "The Painter" are from *Some Trees* (New Haven: Yale University Press, 1956). "Farm Implements and Rutabagas in a Landscape" is from *The Double Dream of Spring* (New York: E.P. Dutton, 1970). "Daffy Duck in Hollywood" is from *Houseboat Days* (New York: Viking, 1977). "The Songs We Know Best" and "37 Haiku" are from *A Wave* (New York: Viking, 1984). "Finnish Rhapsody" is from *April Galleons* (New York: Viking, 1987). "Hotel Lautréamont" is from *Hotel Lautréamont* (New York: Alfred A. Knopf, 1992). ". . . by an Earthquake" is from *Can You Hear, Bird* (New York: Farrar, Straus & Giroux, 1995). "The Dong with the Luminous Nose" is from *Wakefulness* (New York: Farrar, Straus & Giroux, 1998).

"Europe" and "Idaho" are from *The Tennis Court Oath* (Middletown, CT: Wesleyan University Press, 1962). Copyright © 1962, 1997, 2008 by John Ashbery. All rights reserved. Used by arrangement with Wesleyan University Press.

"They Knew What They Wanted" is from *Planisphere* (New York: Ecco, 2009). "Haunted Ride" and "Impermeable" are from *Commotion of the Birds* (New York: Ecco, 2016). Copyright © 2009 and 2016 by John Ashbery. All rights reserved. Used by arrangement with Ecco.

*

The editor gratefully acknowledges the crucial contributions of the individuals who made this volume possible: At Tibor de Nagy: Andrew Arnot, Salvatore Schiciano, and Eric Brown; at Rizzoli: Charles Miers, Margaret Rennolds Chace, and Ellen Nidy; as well as John Yau, Emily Skillings, and especially John Ashbery and David Kermani, for their extraordinary help and patience throughout the evolution of this project.

First published in the United States of America in 2018 by
Rizzoli Electa
A Division of Rizzoli International Publications, Inc.
300 Park Avenue South, New York, NY 10010
www.rizzoliusa.com

© 2018 Skira Rizzoli International Publications, Inc.
Poems and collages © 1948, 1953, 1956, 1962, 1965, 1970, 1977, 1984, 1987, 1992, 1995, 1997, 1998, 2008, 2009, 2016, 2017, 2018 John Ashbery. All rights reserved.
Introduction © 2018 John Yau
Interview © 2018 John Yau and John Ashbery
Preface, compilation, and book design © 2018 Mark Polizzotti

FRONT OF JACKET: Promenade (detail, p. 71); BACK OF JACKET: Late for School (detail, p. 21); FRONT COVER: Acrobats (detail, p. 56); INTERIOR DETAILS: p. 2: from *Corona* (p. 80); p. 4: from *Northern Lights* (p. 124); p. 6: from *Gotcha!* (p. 67); p. 37: from *The Mail in Russia* (p. 83); p. 126: from *Minnie from Maude* (p. 104).

2018 2019 2020 2021 2022 / 10 9 8 7 6 5 4 3 2 1

ISBN-13: 978-0-8478-6056-2

Library of Congress Control Number: 2017956512

Printed and bound in China

Distributed to the U.S. trade by Random House